Signs in My World

Signs at the Pool

By Mary Hill

Children's Press®
A Division of Scholastic Inc.
New York / Toronto / London / Auckland / Sydney
Mexico City / New Delhi / Hong Kong
Danbury, Connecticut

Photo Credits: Cover and all photos by Maura B. McConnell
Contributing Editor: Jennifer Silate
Book Design: Erica Clendening and Michelle Innes

Library of Congress Cataloging-in-Publication Data

Hill, Mary, 1977—
    Signs at the pool / by Mary Hill.
    p. cm. — (Signs in my world)
    Includes index.
    Summary: On a trip to the pool with her mother, Maria notices the
    various signs that help them, including one that lists the pool hours,
    two that state safety rules, and several that show the depth of the
    water.
    ISBN 0-516-24275-X (lib. bdg.) — ISBN 0-516-24367-5 (pbk.)
    1. Swimming—Safety measures—Juvenile literature. 2. Swimming
    pools—Juvenile literature. 3. Signs and signboards—Juvenile
    literature. [1. Swimming—Safety measures. 2. Swimming pools. 3. Signs
    and signboards.] I. Title. II. Series.

    GV838.53.S24 H55 2003
    797.2'1'083--dc21
                                                        2002011317

Contents

1 The Pool 4

2 No Running 10

3 No Diving 14

4 New Words 22

5 To Find Out More 23

6 Index 24

7 About the Author 24

My name is Maria.

Mom and I are going to swim in the **pool** today.

There is a **sign**.

It says, "Pool Open from 11:00 A.M. to 8:00 P.M."

**Pool Open
from
11:00 A.M. to 8:00 P.M.**

The pool is open until 8:00 P.M. tonight.

It is now 1:00 P.M.

We have lots of time to swim.

9

This sign says, "No Running."

11

I walk around the pool.

I am **careful** not to fall.

13

This sign says, "No **Diving**."

I use the stairs to get into the pool.

15

There is also a sign by the pool.

It says, "3."

The sign means that the water here is 3 feet deep.

The water is not too deep for me to swim.

19

There is a sign that says, "4."

Four feet of water is too deep for me to swim.

The signs at the pool are very helpful.

New Words

careful (**kair**-fuhl) to pay close attention

diving (**dive**-ing) going into water with
your head and arms first

pool (**pool**) something filled with water
and used for swimming

sign (**sine**) a public notice giving
information

To Find Out More

Books
Safety at the Swimming Pool
by Lucia Raatma
Capstone Press

Swimming
by Kirk Bizley
Heinemann Library

Web Site
Swim-City.com
http://www.swim-city.com/kidscourt.php3
Play fun swimming games on this Web site.

Index

pool, 4, 6, 8, 12, 14, 16, 20

sign, 6, 10, 14, 16, 18, 20

swim, 4, 8, 18, 20

water, 18, 20

About the Author
Mary Hill writes and edits children's books.

Reading Consultants

Kris Flynn, Coordinator, Small School District Literacy, The San Diego County Office of Education

Shelly Forys, Certified Reading Recovery Specialist, W.J. Zahnow Elementary School, Waterloo, IL

Sue McAdams, Former President of the North Texas Reading Council of the IRA, and Early Literacy Consultant, Dallas, TX